This book belongs to:
(Este libro pertenece a:)

To Leigh,
Hope you enjoy reading this book to your brother and your stuffed animals!
With love,
Diana Lee ♡

"Colors! Colors! Where can you be?

Why are you totally hiding from me?

Mommy told me to look all around,

but who are you and where can you be found?"

"¡Colores! ¡Colores! ¿Dónde estarán?

¿Por qué se esconden de mí?

Mamá me dijo que buscara por todas partes, pero

¿quiénes son y dónde están?"

2

"We are over here," they say.

"We are colors and we are coming your way.

Let us come and say hi.

We are the colors you are trying to spy."

"Estamos aquí," dicen ellos.

"Somos los colores y vamos a tu encuentro.

Permítenos saludarte.

Somos los colores que estás

tratando de encontrar."

4

"I am red! I sleep on your bed."

"¡Soy el rojo! Yo duermo en tu cama."

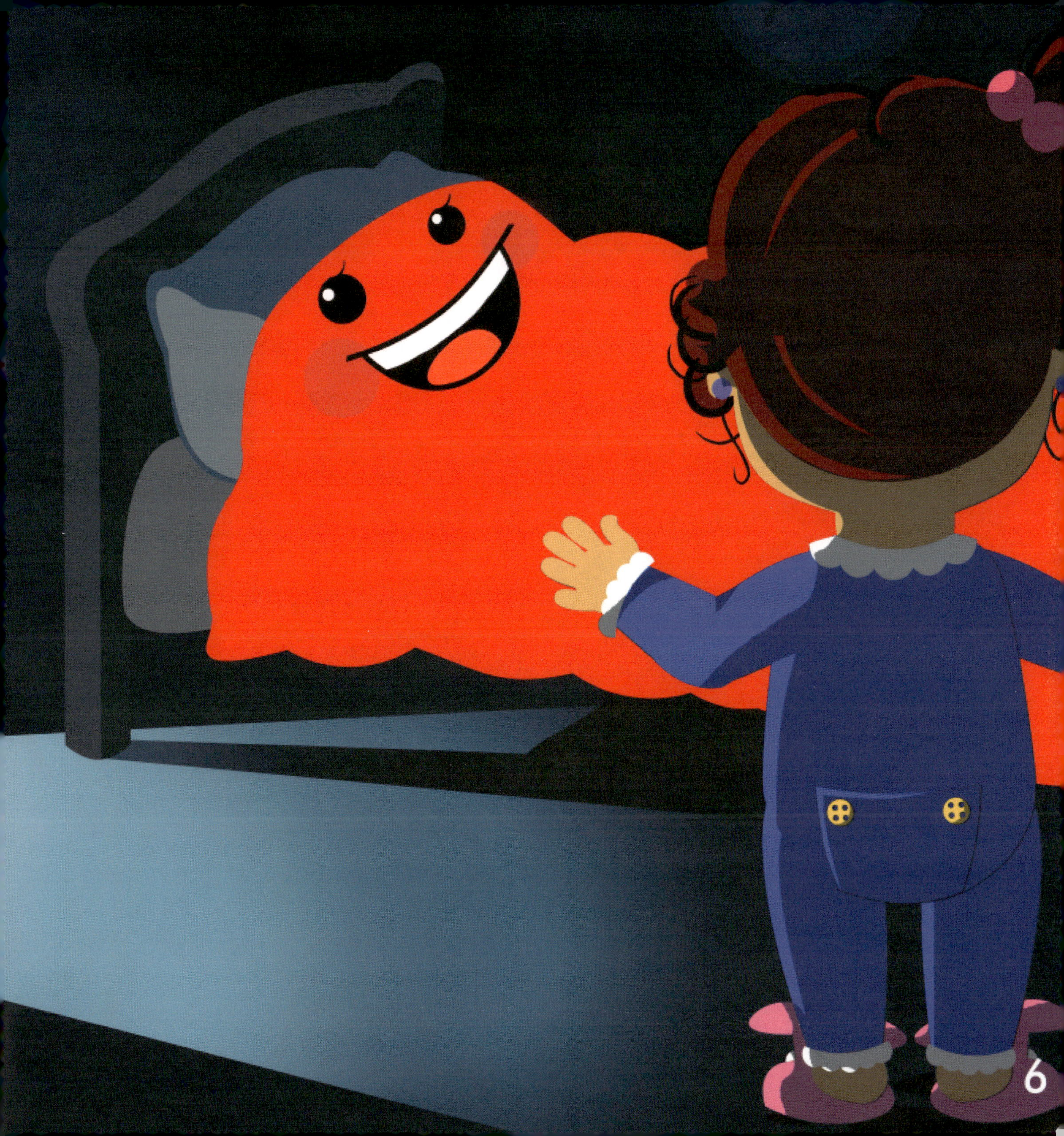

"I am blue! I go on your shoe."

"¡Soy el azul! Yo estoy en tu zapato."

8

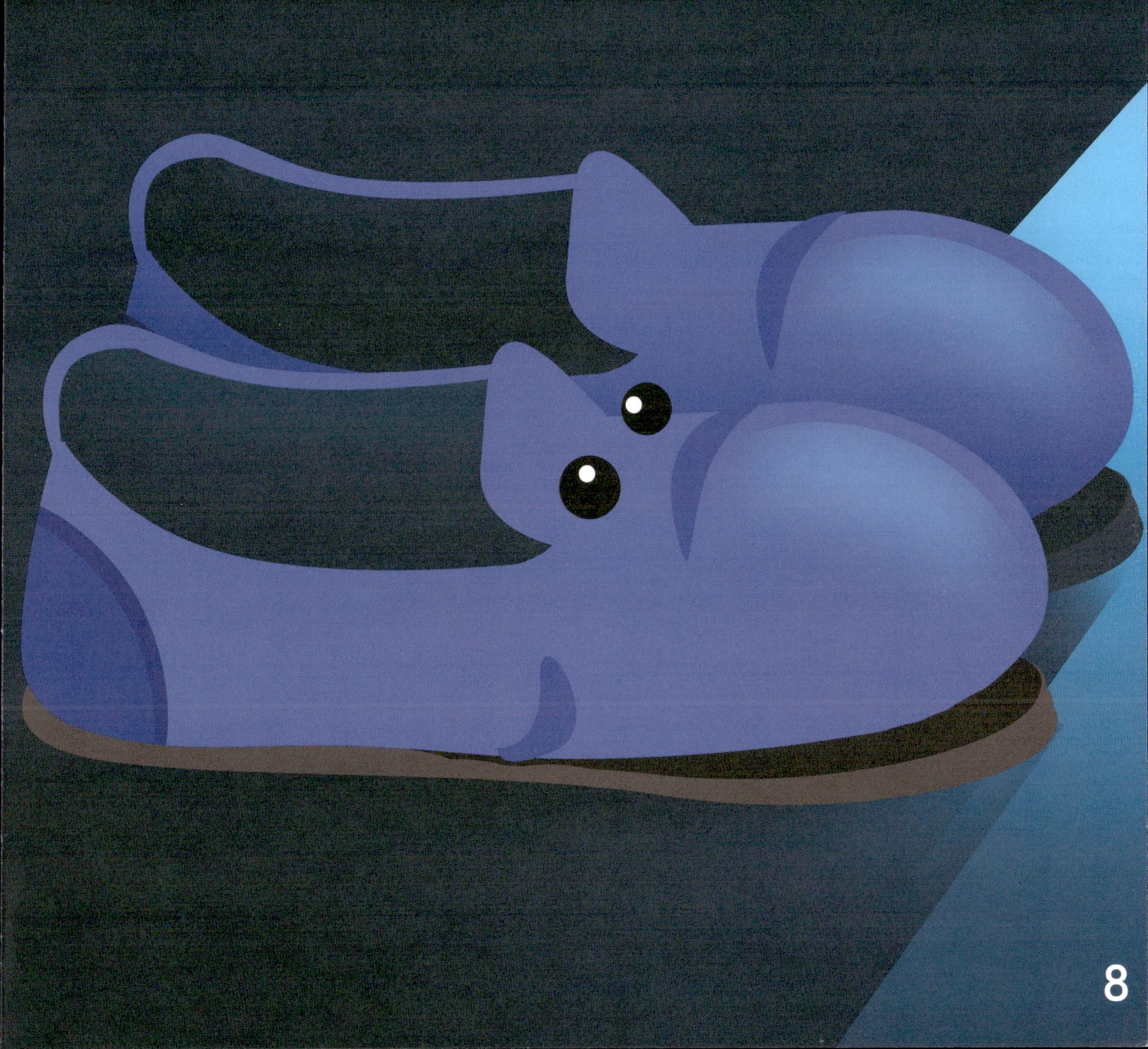

"I am yellow!

I am a bright and friendly fellow."

"¡Soy el amarillo!

Yo soy un compañero brillante y amigable."

10

"But wait there is more…"

"Pero, espera, somos más…"

12

"Purple, orange, and green

are waving by the closet door."

"El violeta, el naranja y el verde

te saludan junto a la puerta del armario."

14

"So as you can see,

we are all around you DLee."

"Así que, como puedes ver,

estamos todos a tu alrededor, DLee."

16

"Now close your eyes and get ready for bed.

We will see you in the morning, sleepy head!"

"Ahora, cierra los ojos y prepárate para dormir.

¡Hasta mañana, dormilona!"

18

19

If you liked this book, check out DLee in:

(Si te gustó este libro, echa un vistazo a DLee en:)

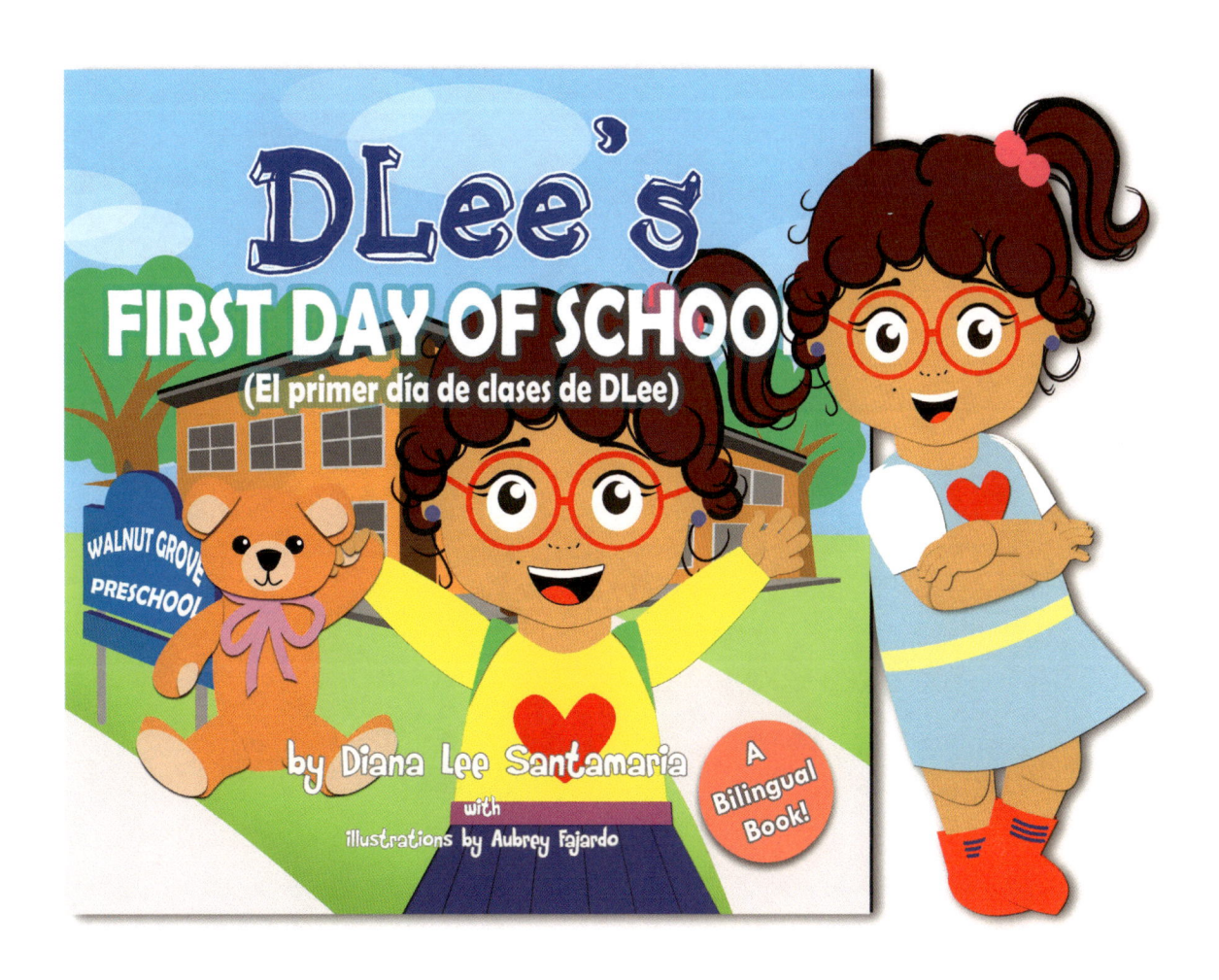

DLee's FIRST DAY OF SCHOOL
(El primer día de clases de DLee)

by Diana Lee Santamaria
with illustrations by Aubrey Fajardo

A Bilingual Book!

www.dleesworld.com

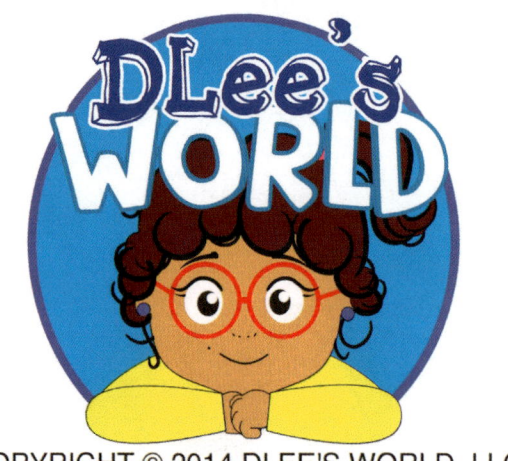

COPYRIGHT © 2014 DLEE'S WORLD, LLC.
ALL RIGHTS RESERVED.

Made in the USA
Charleston, SC
04 April 2016